W9-ATT-472

Cycles in Nature™

THE ROCK CYCLE

Suzanne Slade

The Rosen Publishing Group's
PowerKids Press™
New York

To Mrs. Leffelman, who is older than rocks (and dirt)

Published in 2007 by The Rosen Publishing Group, Inc.
29 East 21st Street, New York, NY 10010

Copyright © 2007 by The Rosen Publishing Group, Inc.

First Edition

Editor: Joanne Randolph
Book Design: Greg Tucker
Photo Researcher: Jeffrey Wendt

Illustrations pp. 6, 10, 12, 14, 16, 18, 20 by Greg Tucker.
Photo Credits: Cover, p. 1 © Krafft / Photo Researchers, Inc.; p. 4 © SPL / Photo Researchers, Inc.; p. 5 © Dennis Flaherty / Photo Researchers, Inc.; pp. 7, 8, 21 (right) © Joyce Photographics / Photo Researchers, Inc.; p. 9 © Andrew J. Martinez / Photo Researchers, Inc.; p. 11 © Stephen & Donna O'Meara / Volcano Watch Int'l / Photo Researchers, Inc.; p. 13 © Fridmar Damm/zefa/Corbis; p. 15 © Frank Lukasseck/zefa/Corbis; p. 17 (left) © Louie Psihoyos/Corbis; p. 17 (right) © Alfred Pasieka / Photo Researchers, Inc.; p. 19 (left) © John Kaprielian / Photo Researchers, Inc.; p. 19 (right) © Dirk Wiersma / Photo Researchers, Inc.; p. 21 (left) © George D. Lepp/Corbis.

Library of Congress Cataloging-in-Publication Data

Slade, Suzanne.
  The rock cycle / Suzanne Slade.— 1st ed.
      p. cm. — (Cycles in nature)
  Includes bibliographical references and index.
  ISBN 1-4042-3493-4 (library binding : alk. paper) — ISBN 1-4042-2202-2 (pbk. : alk. paper) — ISBN 1-4042-2392-4 (six pack : alk. paper)
  1. Petrology—Juvenile literature. 2. Geochemical cycles—Juvenile literature. I. Title. II. Cycles in nature (PowerKids Press)
  QE432.2.S63 2007
  552—dc22
                                        2006008314

Manufactured in the United States of America

Contents

The Changing Earth

Your home, the **planet** Earth, is more than 4.5 **billion** years old. Earth is mostly made of rock. Rocks form mountains, ocean floors, and beautiful coasts. In fact the entire outside layer of Earth is made of rock. This outer layer is called the crust. Earth's crust is between 3 and 43 miles (5–69 km) thick. The crust is made up of about 15 large pieces called tectonic plates. These plates fit together like a giant, Earth-sized puzzle!

The tectonic plates on Earth's surface are slowly shifting, or

The red lines on this map show the location of Earth's tectonic plates. The motion of the plates plays a large part in the rock cycle and in the shaping and reshaping of Earth's crust.

moving. As these plates shift, they create mountains and **volcanoes**. They also make mountains under the ocean called ridges. Rocks inside the crust are changing, too. The shaping and reshaping of Earth's crust is part of a **process** called the rock **cycle**.

Cycle Facts

The tectonic plates in Earth's crust move very slowly. Most plates shift only about 2 inches (5 cm) in a year. That's slower than the hair on your head grows!

The Rock Cycle

Earth's crust is made of rocks of different sizes, shapes, and colors. All Earth's rocks belong to three main groups. These are igneous, sedimentary, and metamorphic. Each kind of rock can change into any other type of rock. For example, over time an igneous rock can become a sedimentary or metamorphic rock. It takes thousands or even millions of years

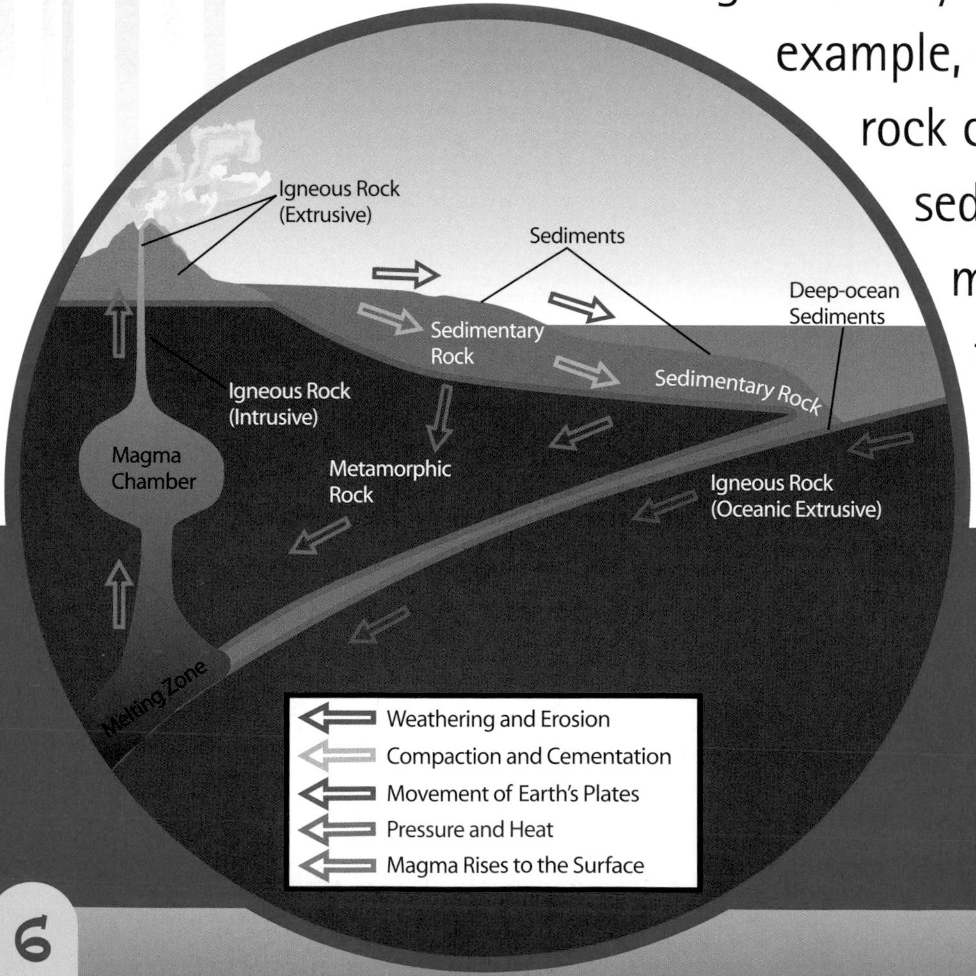

Igneous Rock
(Extrusive)

Sediments

Deep-ocean
Sediments

Sedimentary
Rock

Sedimentary Rock

Igneous Rock
(Intrusive)

Magma
Chamber

Metamorphic
Rock

Igneous Rock
(Oceanic Extrusive)

Melting Zone

Weathering and Erosion
Compaction and Cementation
Movement of Earth's Plates
Pressure and Heat
Magma Rises to the Surface

This picture shows the parts of the rock cycle. The colored arrows show the different forces in action above and below Earth's surface that cause rocks to change form.

Here are three different kinds of rock. On the left is sandstone, a sedimentary rock. In the middle is granite, an igneous rock. On the right is schist, a metamorphic rock.

Sandstone (Sedimentary)

Granite (Igneous)

Schist (Metamorphic)

for one rock to change into a different type of rock. Earth's rock cycle is the process that changes one kind of rock into another.

Scientists determine a rock's type based on the way it was formed. A rock can be changed into a new kind of rock by heat, **pressure,** wind, rain, and other processes in nature. Earth's rocks are always changing in the endless rock cycle.

Cycle Facts

Earth is made of sedimentary, igneous, and metamorphic rock. The Moon is made entirely of igneous rock, though. The dark spots you see on the Moon are flat areas made of an igneous rock called basalt. The Moon's white places are hills made of igneous rocks like anorthosite, norite, and troctolite.

What Is a Rock?

Did you ever save a rock you found because you liked how it looked or felt? The way a rock looks and feels depends on its composition and texture. The composition of a rock is what makes it up. All rocks are made of bits of minerals called grains. Minerals are solids that form from nonliving things. Some rocks are also made from decayed, or rotted, plants or animals. The types of minerals or other matter in a rock help scientists identify, or recognize, the rock. A rock's texture refers to the

Pumice rocks are igneous rocks formed when lava cools on Earth's surface. The many holes in pumice were air bubbles in the lava. Because of all these holes, pumice is a very light rock that can often float in water.

Coal is an example of a rock that is made of decayed living plants or animals.

way it feels. Texture is based on the shape and size of its grains. A rock made of large grains is bumpy or coarse. A rock with small grains feels fine or smooth. Earth's rocks continually change in the rock cycle. The composition and texture of rocks change, too.

Cycle Facts

Shale rock has a very soft and smooth texture. It is made of fine grains of mud and clay. Limestone rock has a texture that is coarse. Most limestone is made of small shells and bones of animals that once lived in the ocean.

Igneous Rock

The rock cycle has no beginning or end. However, you could start following the rock cycle in the layer beneath the crust called the mantle. Hot, melted rock called magma is found in the mantle. The magma rises through cracks in the crust. It can sometimes even break through to Earth's surface as lava. When magma cools it creates igneous rock. Igneous rock that forms below Earth's surface is called

Igneous Rock
(Extrusive)

Sediments

Deep-o
Sedimen

Sedimentary
Rock

Sedimentary Rock

Igneous Rock
(Intrusive)

Magma
Chamber

Metamorphic
Rock

Igneous Rock
(Oceanic Extrusive)

Melting Zone

Movement of Earth's Plates
Magma Rises to the Surface

This picture highlights the part of the rock cycle where igneous rocks are formed. Can you see where the magma rises and breaks through as lava on Earth's surface?

Kilauea Volcano in Hawaii is the most active volcano in the world. Here you can see lava from Kilauea flowing toward the sea. As the lava cools and hardens it becomes basalt.

intrusive. Igneous rock that forms on Earth's surface is called extrusive.

The texture of an igneous rock depends on how quickly magma or lava cools. If magma cools slowly it creates coarse rock. Intrusive rock is coarse because the rock surrounding the hot magma causes it to cool slowly. Lava cools quickly on Earth's surface and creates fine-textured rocks like **basalt**.

Cycle Facts

The islands of Hawaii are made of the black igneous rock called basalt. The islands formed over thousands of years as lava leaked out of a hole in one of the plates in Earth's crust and slowly piled up. Today a new island named Loihi is forming under the ocean. Scientists think it will appear above water in another 100,000 years.

Weathering and Erosion

During the rock cycle, processes in nature help change rocks. Weathering is one process that plays a part in the rock cycle. Weathering breaks the igneous, metamorphic, and sedimentary rocks on Earth's surface into smaller pieces. Water, ice, sunlight, wind, and **gravity** cause rocks to weather. Have you ever noticed how objects that are made of rock, such as stone walls and buildings, have small areas that are missing? This is due to weathering. Erosion moves pieces of weathered rock, called sediments

ock
ve)

Sediments

Deep-ocea
Sediments

Sedimentary
Rock

us Rock
sive)

Sedimentary Rock

Metamorphic
Rock

Igneous Rock
(Oceanic Extrusive)

← Weathering and Erosion

This picture shows how weathering and erosion play a part in the rock cycle. The blue arrows show that the forces of weathering and erosion move sediments. As the sediments are put down, or deposited, they form layers.

Weathering and erosion smooth and cut rock. These beautiful arches in Utah were created by wind and water over a long time. The arches are made of sandstone, which is a sedimentary rock.

or clasts, to new places. Wind, water, and ice move sediments across land or wash them down rivers. A large amount of sediment often collects and forms **layers** in places such as the ocean floor. Over time layers of different sizes and kinds of sediments build up.

Cycle Facts

The thin layer of dirt, or soil, on Earth's surface is created by weathering. Soil is mostly made of tiny pieces of rock that have weathered from larger rocks. This rock is mixed with decayed, or rotted, plants and animals.

Compaction and Cementation

As the rock cycle continues, the top layers of sediment press down on the lower layers. The sedimentary layers become compacted, or pushed together. Also, minerals from rocks that have **dissolved** in water form a type of glue. This glue cements, or binds, the layer of sediments together. As these compacted and cemented layers of sediments harden, they turn into sedimentary rock. Sedimentary rock is the most common rock found on Earth's surface.

Igneous Rock (Extrusive)

Sediments

Deep-ocean Sediment

Sedimentary Rock

Sedimentary Rock

Igneous Rock (Intrusive)

Metamorphic Rock

Igneous Rock (Oceanic Extrusive)

Compaction and Cementation

The green arrows in this picture show that layers of sediment are compacted and cemented together to form sedimentary rock.

Here you can see the layers in these sedimentary rock formations in Utah. Even if you do not live in Utah, you may have seen strata lines in a gravel pit, or in large rocks that were cut when a new road was built.

The most noticeable feature about sedimentary rock is its stratification, or layering. Scientists call the colored layers in sedimentary rock strata. Strata are formed as different types of sediment are deposited, or left behind, over time.

Cycle Facts

You can see more than 20 different kinds of sedimentary rock in the colorful layers of rock in the Grand Canyon.

The Three Types of Sedimentary Rock

Three types of sedimentary rocks are created from different kinds of sediments. Clastic sedimentary rock is produced from sediments of tiny minerals and rocks called clasts. The clasts can be small grains of sand and form sandstone. The clast can also be larger pieces of rocks that are cemented together. This kind of sedimentary rock is called a conglomerate. It is easy to see the igneous, metamorphic, and sedimentary rocks that helped make a conglomerate!

Chemical sedimentary rock forms from a mixture of minerals

Sediments

Deep-ocean Sediments

Sedimentary Rock

Sedimentary Rock

:k

etamorphic
:k

Igneous Rock
(Oceanic Extrusive)

Can you see the sedimentary rock in this picture? Though sedimentary rock covers most of Earth's crust, it actually only makes up about 5 percent of the whole crust. It basically forms a thin layer over large areas, but beneath it are igneous and metamorphic rocks.

dissolved in water. The minerals **crystallize** into thin layers to create sedimentary rock. Halite and gypsum are chemical sedimentary rocks. **Organic** rock is the third type of sedimentary rock. It has small bits of dead plants and animals in its layers. Limestone is an organic sedimentary rock.

This is a close-up look at a piece of gypsum. Gypsum is a chemical sedimentary rock.

This fossil has been kept safe by the layers of sediment that formed over it and became rock over a long time. This fossil is Archaeopteryx, which lived about 150 million years ago.

Cycle Facts

Sometimes larger pieces of dead plants and animals are trapped in the layers of sedimentary rock. These plant and animal remains are preserved, or kept, in the rock. Remains of living things that are found in sedimentary rocks are called fossils. Scientists use fossils to learn about plants or animals that lived long ago, such as dinosaurs, and their habitats or homes.

Metamorphic Rock

Igneous and sedimentary rock can become metamorphic rock in the rock cycle. "Metamorphic" means "changed shape." Metamorphic rock forms during **contact** or **regional** metamorphism. Contact metamorphism occurs when magma escapes into Earth's crust. This magma heats surrounding rocks to a **temperature** of 302° F–1,832° F (150° C–1,000° C). These temperatures cause the rock to go through a chemical change and become a new kind of rock. Regional metamorphism happens

Sedimentary Rock

Igneous Rock (Intrusive)

gma amber

Metamorphic Rock

Pressure and Heat

The purple arrows here show that high heat and pressure cause metamorphic rocks to form. The pressure and heat might be caused by the tectonic plates moving, or from the weight of matter above pressing down. Heat could also come from magma or lava that heats the rocks a lot and change their makeup, but not enough to melt them.

when pieces of Earth's crust push against each other. This creates high temperatures and pressures.

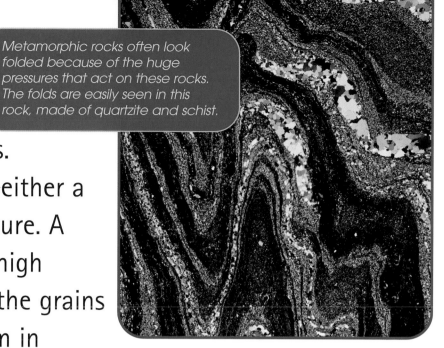

Metamorphic rocks often look folded because of the huge pressures that act on these rocks. The folds are easily seen in this rock, made of quartzite and schist.

A metamorphic rock has either a foliated or nonfoliated texture. A foliated rock is created by high pressure. Pressure flattens the grains in a rock and arranges them in straight lines. A nonfoliated rock forms under high pressure and temperature. These forces cause its grains to grow and move closer together.

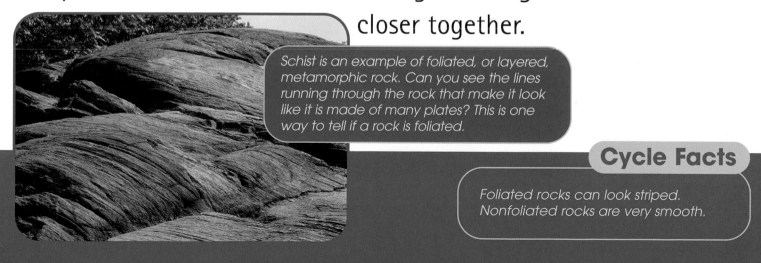

Schist is an example of foliated, or layered, metamorphic rock. Can you see the lines running through the rock that make it look like it is made of many plates? This is one way to tell if a rock is foliated.

Cycle Facts

Foliated rocks can look striped. Nonfoliated rocks are very smooth.

Many Paths in the Rock Cycle

As a rock travels through the rock cycle, there are several paths it could take. For example, an underground igneous rock might be heated by nearby magma and turn into metamorphic rock. Over time this rock can rise to Earth's surface. It then weathers and erodes. Over time it becomes sedimentary rock. Then this rock could sink and melt into a magma pool. When the magma cools, it becomes an intrusive igneous rock again.

That same igneous rock could take another path and move to

Igneous Rock
(Extrusive)

Sediments

Deep-ocean
Sediments

Sedimentary
Rock

Sedimentary Rock

Igneous Rock
(Intrusive)

Magma
Chamber

Metamorphic
Rock

Igneous Rock
(Oceanic Extrusive)

Melting Zone

⬅ Weathering and Erosion
⬅ Compaction and Cementation
⬅ Movement of Earth's Plates
⬅ Pressure and Heat
⬅ Magma Rises to the Surface

Without the rock cycle, we would not have the beautiful mountains, canyons, or beaches that make up Earth's surface. No matter what path a rock takes through the rock cycle, it is playing an important part in the shaping and reshaping of Earth.

Earth's surface and weather into a sedimentary rock. Then it could be pressed into a metamorphic rock by Earth's shifting plates. Next it might be melted by magma and shoot to Earth's surface as lava. Then it becomes extrusive igneous rock. Whatever the path, rocks are always changing.

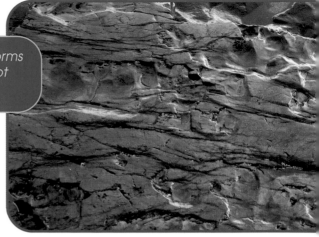

Shale is a sedimentary rock that forms from mud. It is a soft rock and is not very strong.

When shale is heated or pressed enough, it forms the metamorphic rock called slate. Shale (above) and slate are two steps in one rock's path through the rock cycle.

Cycle Facts

Earth's mountains are formed when its tectonic plates bump together and push land up. Nearly every mountain on Earth is made of metamorphic rock. The tallest mountain in the world, Mount Everest, is made of two types of metamorphic rock called schist and gneiss, along with other rock.

Rocks in Our World

Throughout history people have used rocks to make useful and beautiful things. For example, Native Americans made arrowheads out of a black igneous rock called obsidian. Although you may not realize it, you depend on igneous, sedimentary, and metamorphic rocks everyday.

Granite is a strong igneous rock that is used make buildings. The walls of the Empire State Building in New York are made of granite. A sedimentary rock called limestone is found in cement. The most commonly used metamorphic rock is marble. Marble has a shiny surface and is easy to cut. Some people use marble to make floors, walls in bathrooms, sinks, and table tops. The rocks we use today have formed from other types of rocks in Earth's never-ending rock cycle.

Cycle Facts

Part of the 4,000-mile-long (6,400 km) Great Wall of China is made of granite.

Glossary

basalt (buh-SALT) A hard, dark-colored rock.

billion (BIL-yun) A thousands millions.

chemical (KEH-mih-kul) Having to do with matter that can be mixed with other matter to cause changes.

contact (KON-takt) The touching or meeting of people or things.

crystallize (KRIS-tuh-lyz) To form into a solid as liquid disappears from a mixture.

cycle (SY-kul) A course of events that happens in the same order over and over.

dissolved (dih-ZOLVD) To seemed to have disappeared when mixed with a liquid.

granite (GRA-nit) Melted rock that cooled and hardened beneath Earth's surface.

gravity (GRA-vih-tee) The natural force that causes objects to move toward the center of Earth.

layers (LAY-erz) Many thicknesses of something.

organic (or-GA-nik) Made from plants or animals.

planet (PLA-net) A large object, such as Earth, that moves around the Sun.

pressure (PREH-shur) A force that pushes on something.

process (PRAH-ses) A set of actions done in a certain order.

regional (REEJ-nuhl) Having to do with a certain area.

temperature (TEM-pruh-cher) How hot or cold something is.

volcanoes (vol-KAY-nohz) Openings in the surface of Earth that sometimes shoot up a hot liquid rock called lava.

Index

Web Sites

Due to the changing nature of Internet links, PowerKids Press has developed an online list of Web sites related to the subject of this book. This site is updated regularly. Please use this link to access the list:
http://www.powerkidslinks.com/cin/rock/